LIFE

HarperCollins books may be purchased for educational, business, or sales promotional
use. For information, please write: Special Markets Department, HarperCollins
Publishers, 10 East 53rd Street, New York, NY 10022.

Published in agreement with Sant Jordi Asociados Agencia Literaria, S.L., Barcelona,
Spain. www.santjordi-asociados.com

Text selection and editing: Marcia Botelho
Illustrations: Anne Kristin Hagesæther
Photographs © Boris Buzin
Graphic designer: Lene Stangebye Geving
Production manager: Ragnar Sørum

www.paulocoelho.com

Library of Congress Cataloging-in-Publication Data is available upon request.

ISBN: 978-0-06-137481-4

10 11   PHX   10 9 8 7 6 5 4

PAULO COELHO

LIFE

Selected Quotations

HarperCollins*Publishers*

LIFE

What is this force that drives us far from the comfort of the familiar and makes us take up challenges instead, even though we know that the glory of this world is only transitory? I believe this impulse is called the search for the meaning of life. Over many years of seeking a definitive answer to this question in books, art and science, and in both the dangerous and easy paths I have followed, I have found many answers. I am convinced now that a definitive answer will never be given to us in this life, but that, at the last, at the moment when we stand once more before the Creator, we will understand each opportunity that was offered to us.

ACCEPTANCE SPEECH DELIVERED TO THE BRAZILIAN ACADEMY OF LETTERS

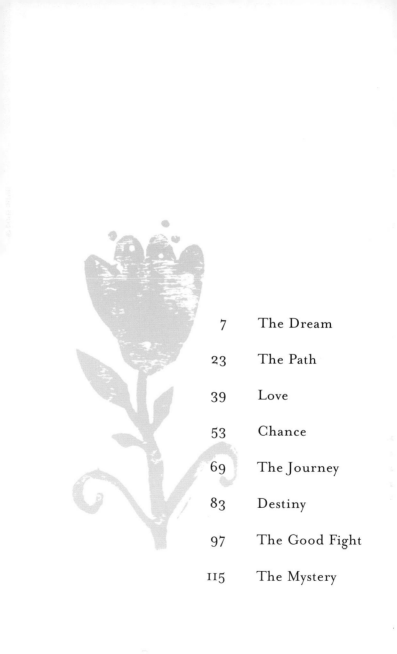

The Dream

The closer you get to your dream,
the more your Personal Legend
becomes your real reason for living.

THE ALCHEMIST

When you want something,
the whole Universe conspires
to help you realize your desire.

THE ALCHEMIST

Only one thing makes a dream impossible:
the fear of failure.

THE ALCHEMIST

Sometimes happiness is a blessing,
but, generally, it is a conquest.
Each day's magic moment
helps us to change and sends us off
in search of our dreams.

**BY THE RIVER PIEDRA
I SAT DOWN AND WEPT**

A search always starts with Beginner's Luck
and ends with the Test of the Conqueror.

THE ALCHEMIST

Love will never separate a man
from his Personal Legend.

THE ALCHEMIST

The Good Fight is the one that we fight
in the name of our dreams,
it was brought from the battlefields
into our very selves.

THE PILGRIMAGE

Sometimes it is impossible to stop the river of life.

THE ALCHEMIST

We cannot all see dreams in the same way.

THE ALCHEMIST

The search for happiness
is more important than the need for pain.

ELEVEN MINUTES

Emotions are wild horses.
It is not explanations that carry us forward,
but our will to go on.

BRIDA

The fear of suffering is worse than suffering itself.
And no heart ever suffered
when it went in search of its dreams.

THE ALCHEMIST

All battles in life serve to teach us something,
even the battles we lose.

THE FIFTH MOUNTAIN

Dreams nourish the soul
just as food nourishes the body.
The pleasure of the search
and of adventure feeds our dreams.

THE PILGRIMAGE

Defeat exists, but not suffering.
A true warrior knows that when he loses a battle
he is improving the skill
with which he wields a sword.
He will be able to fight more skilfully next time.

**BY THE RIVER PIEDRA
I SAT DOWN AND WEPT**

It is precisely the possibility of realizing a dream
that makes life interesting.
THE ALCHEMIST

The world lies in the hands of those
who have the courage to dream and
who take the risk of living out their dreams
— each according to his or her own talent.

THE VALKYRIES

If you have a past with which you feel dissatisfied,
then forget it, now.
Imagine a new story for your life and believe in it.
Focus only on the moments
when you achieved what you desired,
and that strength will help you
to get what you want.

THE FIFTH MOUNTAIN

To each of man's ages
the Lord gives its own anxieties.

THE FIFTH MOUNTAIN

The first indication
that we are killing our dreams is lack of time.
The second indication
that our dreams are dead is certainty.
The third indication
that our dreams are dead is peace.

THE PILGRIMAGE

Body and soul need new challenges.

THE MANUAL OF THE WARRIOR OF LIGHT

When someone wants something then they should
be aware that they are taking a risk. But this is
precisely what makes life interesting.

THE PILGRIMAGE

The only way to save our dreams
is by being generous with ourselves.

THE PILGRIMAGE

As soon as people decide to confront a problem,
they realize that they are far more capable
than they thought they were.

THE ZAHIR

On each and every one of these 365 days,
I will look at everyone and everything
as if for the first time,
especially at the smallest things.

CHRONICLE — AS IF FOR THE FIRST TIME

It's one thing for the entire universe
to conspire to make our dreams come true,
it's quite another to set yourself
entirely unnecessary challenges.

CHRONICLE — THE BLINDMAN AND EVEREST

Every moment of searching
is a moment of encounter.

THE ALCHEMIST

Go in search of your Gift.
The more you understand yourself,
the more you will understand the world.

BRIDA

Open your heart
and listen to what it is telling you.
Follow your dreams,
because only a man who is unshamed of himself
can manifest the glory of God.

THE VALKYRIES

We are all growing and changing,
we notice certain weaknesses
that need to be corrected,
and although we may not always
choose the best solution, we carry on regardless.

THE ZAHIR

When we boldly seek love, love reveals itself to us,
and we end up attracting more love.
If one person loves us, everyone loves us.

**BY THE RIVER PIEDRA
I SAT DOWN AND WEPT**

We tend to seek captivity
because we are used to seeing freedom
as something that has neither frontiers
nor responsiblities.

**CHRONICLE
— IN THE RECESSES OF THE HEART**

The inevitable always happens.
We need discipline and patience to overcome it.
And hope.
It isn't a question of placing hope in the future.
It is a question of re-creating our own past.

THE FIFTH MOUNTAIN

Life is made up of simple things
and she had grown weary
of searching for something
quite what she didn't know.

ELEVEN MINUTES

The warrior of light is not afraid
to weep over ancient sorrows
or to feel joy at new discoveries.
When he feels the moment has arrived,
he drops everything
and goes off on some long-dreamed-of adventure.

MANUAL OF THE WARRIOR OF LIGHT

Whenever you want to achieve something,
keep your eyes open,
concentrate and make sure you know exactly what it
is that you want.
No one can hit their target with their eyes closed.

THE DEVIL AND MISS PRYM

Angels are visible to those who accept the light
and break the pact made with darkness.

THE VALKYRIES

The Path

In his or her life,
each person can take one of two attitudes:
to build or to plant.
Builders may take years over their tasks,
but one day they will finish what they are doing.
Then they will stop, hemmed in by their own walls.
Life becomes meaningless
once the building is finished.
Those who plant suffer the storms
and the seasons and rarely rest.
Unlike a building, a garden never stops growing.
And by its constant demands
on the gardener's attentions,
it makes of the gardener's life a great adventure.

BRIDA

In order to have faith in his own path,
a warrior does not need to prove
that someone else's path is wrong.

THE MANUAL OF THE WARRIOR OF LIGHT

At every moment of our lives,
we all have one foot in a fairy tale
and the other in the abyss.

ELEVEN MINUTES

Choosing one path means abandoning others
— if you try to follow every possible path
you will end up following none.

BRIDA

In order to arrive you must follow the signs.
God inscribed on the world
the path that each man must follow.
It is just a matter of reading the inscription
he wrote for you.

THE ALCHEMIST

When you travel towards your objective,
be sure to pay attention to the path.
The path teaches us the best way to arrive
and enriches us while we are traveling along it.

THE PILGRIMAGE

A warrior never gives in to fear
when he is searching for what he needs.
Without love, he is nothing.

THE MANUAL OF THE WARRIOR OF LIGHT

The challenge will not wait.
Life does not look back.
A week is more than enough time for us
to decide whether or not to accept our destiny.

THE DEVIL AND MISS PRYM

Your heart is where your treasure is,
and you must find your treasure
in order to make sense of everything.

THE ALCHEMIST

We always have a tendency to see those things
that do not exist
and to be blind to the great lessons
that are right there before our eyes.

THE PILGRIMAGE

Finding something important in life
does not mean
that you must give up everything else.

BRIDA

The glory of the world is transitory,
and we should not measure our lives by it,
but by the choice we make
to follow our Personal Legend,
to believe in our utopias
and to fight for our dreams.
We are all protagonists of our own lives,
and it is often the anonymous heroes
who leave the deepest mark.

**ACCEPTANCE SPEECH DELIVERED TO
THE BRAZILIAN ACADEMY OF LETTERS**

The only way to make the right decision
is to find out which is the wrong decision,
to examine that other path without fear,
and only then decide.

THE PILGRIMAGE

When we postpone the harvest, the fruit rots,
but when we postpone our problems,
they keep on growing.

THE FIFTH MOUNTAIN

No one day is like another,
each tomorrow has its special miracle,
its magic moment in which old universes
are destroyed and new stars created.

**BY THE RIVER PIEDRA
I SAT DOWN AND WEPT**

Before commencing battle,
the warrior of light
opens his heart and asks God to inspire him.

THE MANUAL OF THE WARRIOR OF LIGHT

It is even more difficult
to define a Path for yourself.
The person who does not make a choice
dies in the eyes of the Lord,
even though he continues to breathe
and to walk about the streets.
For a man has to choose,
therein lies his strength:
in the power of his decisions.

THE FIFTH MOUNTAIN

It hurt when I lost each of the various men
I fell in love with.
Now, though, I am convinced
that no one loses anyone,
because no one owns anyone.
That is the true experience of freedom:
having the most important thing in the world
without owning it.

ELEVEN MINUTES

If you go around promising
what you do not yet have,
you will lose the will to achieve it.

THE ALCHEMIST

Remember: never behave arrogantly
towards the humble
and never behave humbly
towards the arrogant.

CHRONICLE — STORIES ABOUT ARROGANCE

In order to live fully,
it is necessary to be in constant movement,
only then can each day
be different from the last.

THE ZAHIR

The day will come
when those knocking at the door will see it open;
those who ask will receive;
those who weep will be consoled.

THE VALKYRIES

There are moments in life
when we need to trust blindly in intuition.

THE ZAHIR

The distance to the top of the mountain
is always greater than you think.
There is bound to come a moment
when what seemed close is still very far away.

**CHRONICLE
— MANUAL FOR CLIMBING MOUNTAINS**

The simple things
are also the most extraordinary things,
and only the wise can see them.

THE ALCHEMIST

When we are faced by something
that really threatens us,
it's impossible to look around,
even though that is
the safest and most sensible thing to do.

**CHRONICLE
— AT THE END OF THE DARK TUNNEL**

When we train ourselves to win

Victory might give you confidence,
but it must not become a burden to be carried.

**CHRONICLE
— WHEN WE TRAIN OURSELVES TO WIN**

The taste of things recovered
is the sweetest honey we will ever know.

THE ZAHIR

The path involves respect
for all small and subtle things.
Learn to recognize the right moment
to strike the necessary attitudes.

MANUAL OF THE WARRIOR OF LIGHT

When you cease doubting,
you have stopped moving forward.

BRIDA

It is always important to know
when something has reached its end.
Closing circles, shutting doors, finishing chapters,
it doesn't matter what we call it;
what matters is to leave behind us in the past
those moments in life that are over.

THE ZAHIR

Only by accepting our desires
can we have an idea of who we are.

BRIDA

Life is made up of our attitudes.
And there are certain things
that the gods force us to experience.
Their reasons for doing so do not matter,
and there is no point in doing
everything we can to avoid them.

THE FIFTH MOUNTAIN

Love

When we love,
it is not necessary to understand
what is happening outside,
because everything
begins to happen inside us instead.

THE ALCHEMIST

A warrior of light needs love.
Love and affection are part of his nature.
He makes use of solitude,
but is not used by it.

THE MANUAL OF THE WARRIOR OF LIGHT

Love is looking at the same mountains
from different angles.

THE VALKYRIES

Ever since time began,
people have recognized their true Love
by the light in their eyes.

BRIDA

For the warrior of light
there is no such thing as an impossible love.
He is not intimidated by silence,
indifference or rejection.
He knows that, behind the mask of ice
that people wear, there beats a heart of fire.
Without love, he is nothing.

THE MANUAL OF THE WARRIOR OF LIGHT

Accumulating love brings luck,
accumulating hatred brings calamity.

THE MANUAL OF THE WARRIOR OF LIGHT

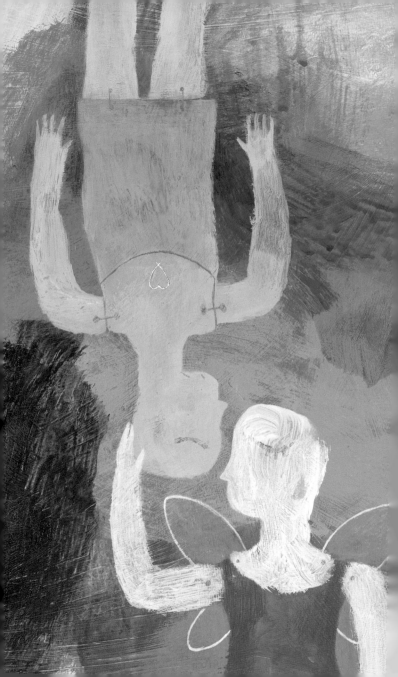

Love is not to be found in someone else,
but in ourselves; we simply awaken it.
But in order to do that, we need the other person.

ELEVEN MINUTES

The strongest love
is the love that can demonstrate its fragility.

ELEVEN MINUTES

He who loves has conquered the world
and has no fear of losing anything.
True love is an act of total surrender.

**BY THE RIVER PIEDRA
I SAT DOWN AND WEPT**

The moment we set off in search of love,
it sets off in search of us. And saves us.

**BY THE RIVER PIEDRA
I SAT DOWN AND WEPT**

Be like the fountain that overflows,
not like the cistern that merely contains.

VERONIKA DECIDES TO DIE

Do not try to explain feelings.
Live everything intensely
and treasure what you feel as a gift from God.

BRIDA

Sometimes an unimportant incident
is capable of turning everything beautiful
into a moment of anxiety.
We insist on seeing the mote in the eye
and forget about the mountains, the fields
and the olive groves.

**BY THE RIVER PIEDRA
I SAT DOWN AND WEPT**

God is love, generosity and forgiveness;
if we believe in this,
we will never allow our weaknesses
to paralyze us.

THE VALKYRIES

Sorrows do not last forever
when we are journeying towards
the thing we have always wanted.

THE FIFTH MOUNTAIN

When you love, things make even more sense.

THE ALCHEMIST

Everything is allowed,
except interrupting a manifestation of love.

THE PILGRIMAGE

We all know people
who try to cover up their kindly gestures
with irony and indifference,
as if love were synonymous
with weakness.

**CHRONICLE
— NOTES FOR A NON-EXISTENT DIARY**

The energy of hatred will get you nowhere;
but the energy of forgiveness,
which reveals itself through love,
will transform your life in a positive way.

THE ZAHIR

During the worst of all my crises,
friends appeared.
Since then, the first thing I do
is ask for help.

CHRONICLE — CRISES AND THEIR TRAPS

No one can desire the love of God
without first knowing human love.

THE FIFTH MOUNTAIN

Love is full of traps.
When it wants to reveal itself,
it shows only its light and
does not let us see the shadows cast by that light.

**BY THE RIVER PIEDRA
I SAT DOWN AND WEPT**

The warrior of light embraces his passions
and enjoys them intensely.
He knows that there is no need
to renounce the pleasures of conquest;
they are part of life and bring joy
to all those who participate in them.

MANUAL OF THE WARRIOR OF LIGHT

Our human condition makes us tend to share
only the best of ourselves,
because we are always searching
for love and approval.

THE ZAHIR

Love is always new.
It doesn't matter if we love once,
twice or ten times in a lifetime,
we will always find ourselves faced
by an unfamiliar situation.

**BY THE RIVER PIEDRA
I SAT DOWN AND WEPT**

The energy that many people call love, is, in fact,
the raw material from which the universe was built.
This energy cannot be manipulated,
it leads us gently forwards,
it contains all we have to learn in this life.

THE ZAHIR

Love is the key to understanding all the mysteries.

BRIDA

The soil needs the seed,
and the seed needs the soil.
One only has meaning with the other.
The same thing happens with human beings.
When male knowledge comes together
with female transformation,
then the great magical union takes place,
which is called Wisdom.

BRIDA

Love means sharing the world with someone else.

THE VALKYRIES

People, since the beginning of time,
have always tried to understand the universe
through love.

BRIDA

When everything has been told and retold
countless times,
when the places I have visited,
the things I have experienced,
the steps I have taken because of her
are all transformed into distant memories,
nothing will remain but pure love.

THE ZAHIR

Anyone who loves must know
how to lose themselves and find themselves again.

**BY THE RIVER PIEDRA
I SAT DOWN AND WEPT**

There is only one sin — lack of love.
Be brave, be capable of loving,
even if love seems a terrible and treacherous thing.
Find joy in love. Find joy in victory.
Follow the dictates of your heart.

THE VALKYRIES

Chance

In this world there is always
one person waiting for another,
be it in the middle of a desert
or in the middle of a big city.
And when those two people pass each other
and their eyes meet,
past and future lose all importance,
and the only thing that exists
is that moment and the incredible certainty
that everything under the sun
was written by the same Hand,
the Hand that awakens Love,
and that makes a twin soul for everyone who works,
rests and seeks treasures under the sun.
Without this our human dreams
would make no sense.

MAKTUB

It is not difficult to rebuild a life.
All we need is to be aware
that we have the same strength we had before,
and to use it in our favor.

THE FIFTH MOUNTAIN

We must make the most of the times
when luck is on our side
and do everything to help it,
just as it is helping us.

THE ALCHEMIST

Life always waits for some crisis to occur
before revealing itself at its most brilliant.

ELEVEN MINUTES

The warrior of light perseveres in his desire,
but knows he must wait for the best moment.

THE MANUAL OF THE WARRIOR OF LIGHT

God judges a tree by its fruits and not by its roots.

THE MANUAL OF THE WARRIOR OF LIGHT

Only those who find life find treasures.

THE ALCHEMIST

The cup of suffering
is not the same size for everyone.

THE MANUAL OF THE WARRIOR OF LIGHT

God, in his infinite wisdom,
hid Hell in the middle of Paradise,
to keep us on our toes.

**BY THE RIVER PIEDRA
I SAT DOWN AND WEPT**

No one knows what is going to happen
in the next few minutes,
and yet people still go forward,
because they have trust,
because they have faith.

BRIDA

The moment that he begins to walk along it,
the warrior of light recognizes the Path.
Each stone, each bend cries welcome to him.
He identifies with the mountains and the streams,
he sees something of his own soul in the plants
and the animals and the birds of the field.
Then, accepting the help of God
and of God's Signs,
he allows his Personal Legend to guide him
towards the tasks that life has reserved for him.

THE MANUAL OF THE WARRIOR OF LIGHT

A warrior accepts defeat.
He does not treat it as a matter of indifference
nor does he try to make a victory out of it.

THE FIFTH MOUNTAIN

The secret lies in the present
— if you pay attention to the present,
you will be able to improve it.
And if you improve the present,
whatever happens afterwards will be better too.
Each day brings us Eternity.

THE ALCHEMIST

She said she was neither happy nor unhappy,
and that was why she couldn't go on.
Each person knows the extent
of their own suffering,
or the total absence of meaning in their lives.

VERONIKA DECIDES TO DIE

When we are high up, everything looks very small.
Our glories and our sadnesses
cease to be important.
We have left whatever we won or lost down below.
From the top of a mountain
you can see how large the world is
and how wide the horizon.

THE FIFTH MOUNTAIN

Warriors of light
frequently ask themselves
what they are doing here.
Very often they believe
their lives have no meaning.
That is why they are warriors of light.
Because they make mistakes.
Because they ask questions.
Because they continue
to look for a meaning.
And, in the end, they will find it.

THE MANUAL OF THE WARRIOR OF LIGHT

When we least expect it,
life sets us a challenge to test our courage
and willingness to change.

THE DEVIL AND MISS PRYM

Everything tells me that
I am about to make a wrong decision,
but making mistakes is just part of life.
What does the world want of me?
Does it want me to take no risks,
to go back where I came from because
I didn't have the courage to say "yes" to life?

ELEVEN MINUTES

Everything tells me that

The two worst tactical errors you can make
are acting too early
and allowing an opportunity to slip by.

CHRONICLE — ACCEPTING PARADOXES

On the way, I meet strong currents, winds
and storms, but I keep rowing, exhausted,
knowing that I have drifted away
from my chosen course
and that the island I was trying to reach
is no longer on my horizon.
I can't turn back, though.

THE ZAHIR

I recovered my immense will to live
when I realized that the meaning of my life
was the one I had chosen for it.

THE FIFTH MOUNTAIN

We are the warriors of light.
With the force of our love and our will
we can change our own destiny
and that of many other people.

THE VALKYRIES

At every moment of our life
there will have been things
that might have happened, but did not.
There are magic moments
that go unnoticed and then, suddenly,
the hand of fate changes our universe.

**BY THE RIVER PIEDRA
I SAT DOWN AND WEPT**

You should try all wines
— of some, take only a sip,
of others, drink the whole bottle.
How can you distinguish one from the other?
By taste.
Only someone who has tasted sour wine
can recognize good wine.

BRIDA

When someone makes a decision,
he is plunging into a rushing torrent
that could lead him to a place
he had never dreamed of going
when he made that decision.

THE ALCHEMIST

When someone finds his path, he cannot be afraid.
He needs to have the courage to go astray.
Disappointments, defeats and despair
are the tools God uses to show us the path.

BRIDA

Everything we need to learn
is always there before us:
we just have to look around us with respect
and attention in order to discover where
God is leading us and
which step we should take next.

THE ZAHIR

You do not drown simply by plunging into water;
you only drown if you stay beneath the surface.

MANUAL OF THE WARRIOR OF LIGHT

I discovered that searching
can be as interesting as finding
— as long as you overcome your fear.

BRIDA

Before certain storms invade our garden,
they send faint messages which,
out of laziness, we ignore.

CHRONICLE — CRISES AND THEIR TRAPS

The Journey

Human beings weren't made solely
to go in search of wisdom,
but also to plough the land, wait for rain,
plant the wheat, harvest the grain, make the bread.

ELEVEN MINUTES

The warrior of light
knows that he is free to choose his desires,
and he makes these decisions with courage,
detachment and — sometimes — with just a touch
of madness.

THE MANUAL OF THE WARRIOR OF LIGHT

When every day seems the same,
it is because we have stopped noticing
the good things that appear in our lives.

THE ALCHEMIST

Everything on the face of the earth
is constantly being transformed
because the Earth is alive and has a Soul.

THE ALCHEMIST

We all live in our own world.
But if you look up at the starry sky,
you'll see that all the different worlds up there
combine to form constellations,
solar systems, galaxies.

VERONIKA DECIDES TO DIE

There are moments in life
when the only possible option is to lose control.

BRIDA

To attain his dream,
the warrior of light needs a strong will
and an enormous capacity for acceptance.

THE MANUAL OF THE WARRIOR OF LIGHT

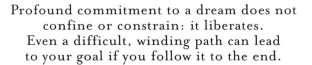

Profound commitment to a dream does not
confine or constrain: it liberates.
Even a difficult, winding path can lead
to your goal if you follow it to the end.

MAKTUB

When there is no turning back,
then we should concern ourselves only
with the best way of going forward.

THE ALCHEMIST

We do not need to know "how" or "where,"
but there is one question
that we should all ask whenever we start anything:
"What am I doing this for?"

THE VALKYRIES

A warrior of light makes decisions.
His soul is as free as the clouds in the sky,
but he is committed to his dream.

THE MANUAL OF THE WARRIOR OF LIGHT

Man needs to choose,
not just accept, his destiny.

THE FIFTH MOUNTAIN

We go out into the world
in search of our dreams and ideals.
Often we store away in some inaccessible place
what is already there
within reach of our hands.

MAKTUB

It is necessary to run risks,
to follow certain paths and to abandon others.
No one can make a choice without feeling fear.

BRIDA

In the search for your destiny,
you will often find yourself obliged
to change direction.

THE FIFTH MOUNTAIN

Suffering, if confronted without fear,
is the great passport to freedom.

ELEVEN MINUTES

Every day of life is a dark night.
No one knows what will happen
in the next moment,
and yet people still go forward.
Because they trust. Because they have faith.

BRIDA

The true companions of a warrior
are beside him always,
during both the difficult times and the easy times.

**CHRONICLE
— THE DECISIONS OF THE WARRIOR**

History will only change
when we are able to use the energy of love,
just as we use the energy of the wind,
the seas and the atom.

THE ZAHIR

From whichever angle you look at the mountain,
it will appear different,
even though it's the same mountain.
That is how it is with all creation
— the many faces of the same god.

THE FIFTH MOUNTAIN

There are moments
when you must be prepared to take a risk,
to do something crazy.

**BY THE RIVER PIEDRA
I SAT DOWN AND WEPT**

Everything is written in the sounds around us.
Man's past, present and future.
A man who does not know how to listen
cannot hear the advice that life is offering us
at every moment.
Only someone who listens to the sound
of the present can make the right decision.

DIARY OF A MAGUS

It was a mistake that set the world in motion
— never be afraid of making a mistake.

BRIDA

Lessons always arrive when you are ready for them,
and if you can read the signs,
you will learn everything you need to know
in order to take the next step.

THE ZAHIR

Those who make promises they fail to keep
end up powerless and frustrated,
and exactly the same fate
awaits those who believe those promises.

THE DEVIL AND MISS PRYM

Courage does not mean an absence of fear,
but the ability not to let yourself
be paralyzed by that fear.

**CHRONICLE
— HAGAKURE AND THE PATH OF THE SAMURAI**

Courage is the most important gift
for anyone seeking to understand
the Language of the World.

THE ALCHEMIST

Carry in your memory,
for the rest of your life,
the good things that came out of your difficulties.
They will serve as a proof of your abilities
and will give you confidence
when you are faced by other obstacles.

MANUAL OF THE WARRIOR OF LIGHT

The first great virtue
of someone seeking the spiritual path
is Courage.

THE VALKYRIES

Destiny

The signs — sometimes imperceptible,
at others very clear — are all around us.
But they require careful interpretation
if they are to be transformed into a road map.

THE MANUAL OF THE WARRIOR OF LIGHT

Seize every opportunity
that life offers you because,
when opportunities go,
they take a long time to come back.

THE FIFTH MOUNTAIN

By changing the way you do routine things
you allow a new man to grow inside you.

THE PILGRIMAGE

A blessing rejected becomes a curse.

THE ALCHEMIST

The noblest thing a human being can experience
is acceptance of the Mystery.

BRIDA

Life moves very fast.
It rushes us from heaven to hell
in a matter of seconds.

ELEVEN MINUTES

Decisions are only the beginning of something.
When someone makes a decision he is, in fact,
plunging into a powerful current
that carries him to a place
he had never even dreamed of
when he made that initial decision.

THE ALCHEMIST

There is no such thing as a single chance.
The Lord gives us many opportunities
during our lifetime.

THE FIFTH MOUNTAIN

Sometimes certain blessings from God
come crashing in through the windows.

BRIDA

Anyone who interferes in the destiny of others
will never discover his own.

THE ALCHEMIST

Wagers and pacts are made with angels
— or with devils.

THE VALKYRIES

The Lord smiles contentedly
because this is what He wants,
that everyone should take responsibility
for their own lives.

THE FIFTH MOUNTAIN

Good and Evil have the same face;
it all depends on when they cross the path
of each individual human being.

THE DEVIL AND MISS PRYM

Whenever we need
to make a very important decision,
it is best to trust to impulse, to passion,
because reason usually tries to
remove us from our dream,
saying that the time is not yet right.
Reason is afraid of defeat,
but intuition enjoys life and its challenges.

**ACCEPTANCE SPEECH DELIVERED TO
THE BRAZILIAN ACADEMY OF LETTERS**

Every person on the face of the earth has a gift.
In some this reveals itself spontaneously,
others have to work to find it.

**BY THE RIVER PIEDRA
I SAT DOWN AND WEPT**

The Gift belongs to whoever chooses to accept it.
It is enough to believe
and not to be afraid to make mistakes.

**BY THE RIVER PIEDRA
I SAT DOWN AND WEPT**

It is important to take
from what we see every day
the secrets that routine
prevents us from perceiving.

THE PILGRIMAGE

Fine words are meaningless
when we come face to face with suffering.

THE FIFTH MOUNTAIN

Enthusiasm is the force
that leads us to the final victory.

THE PILGRIMAGE

When God closes a door,
he opens a window.

**CHRONICLE — CHRISTMAS STORY
— A PLACE IN PARADISE**

For the warrior of light
there are no ends, only means.
Life carries him from unknown to unknown.
Each moment is filled with this thrilling mystery:
the warrior does not know
where he came from or where he is going.

MANUAL OF THE WARRIOR OF LIGHT

I do not know if the desert can be loved,
but it is in the desert that my treasure lies hidden.

THE ALCHEMIST

Men are masters of their destinies.
They are free to make mistakes.
They are free to fly from everything they desire,
even from that which life
so generously places before them.

BRIDA

God's work is to be found
in the smallest details of Creation.

THE ZAHIR

That is why the angels have returned
and need to be heard,
because only they can show us the path,
and no one else.

THE VALKYRIES

The boat is safest when it is in port,
but that is not what boats were built for.

THE DIARY OF A MAGUS

Everyone on the face of the Earth
has a treasure that lies waiting for them.

THE ALCHEMIST

Know that no day is the same as another,
and that each morning
contains its own particular miracle,
its magic moment,
when old universes are destroyed
and new stars created.

**BY THE RIVER PIEDRA
I SAT DOWN AND WEPT**

We all have the right to have doubts
about our task
and even to abandon it occasionally;
the one thing we must not do is to forget it.

THE FIFTH MOUNTAIN

We plunge into the Dark Night with faith,
we fulfill what the ancient alchemists
called our Personal Legend,
and we give ourselves wholly to the moment,
knowing that there is always a hand to guide us;
it is up to us
whether we choose to take that hand or not.

BRIDA

On some nights,
the warrior of light has nowhere to sleep,
on others, he suffers from insomnia.
"That's just how it is," thinks the warrior.
"I was the one who chose to walk this path."

MANUAL OF THE WARRIOR OF LIGHT

I believe that every single day
people are offered the chance
to make the best possible decision
about everything they do.

THE ZAHIR

The Good Fight

In the Good Fight,
attacking or fleeing are part of the struggle;
being paralyzed by fear is not.
The Good Fight is the one we undertake
because our heart wants us to.

THE PILGRIMAGE

No one can avoid defeat.
That is why it is better to lose a few battles
in the fight for your dreams
than to be defeated
without even knowing why you are fighting.

**BY THE RIVER PIEDRA
I SAT DOWN AND WEPT**

No man is an island.
To fight the good fight we need help.

THE PILGRIMAGE

When we renounce our dreams, we find peace
and enjoy a brief period of tranquillity,
but the dead dreams begin to rot inside us
and to infect the whole atmosphere
in which we live.
What we hoped to avoid in the Fight
— disappointment and defeat —
becomes the sole legacy of our cowardice.

THE PILGRIMAGE

The first great virtue of those who seek
the spiritual path is courage.

THE VALKYRIES

It is important never to relax,
however far you have come.

THE ALCHEMIST

Don't try to be brave
when it is enough to be intelligent.

THE PILGRIMAGE

The tests can be harder than one imagined.
But they are necessary in order to learn.
And each of them brings us closer
to the realization of our dreams.

THE MANUAL OF THE WARRIOR OF LIGHT

The warrior of light
calmly goes to his sacred place
and puts on the cloak of faith.
Faith parries all blows.
Faith transforms poison
into crystalline water.

THE MANUAL OF THE WARRIOR OF LIGHT

We're allowed to make a lot of mistakes
in our lives, except the mistake that destroys us.

VERONIKA DECIDES TO DIE

Whoever wants to fight the Good Fight
must regard it as if it were a vast treasure
that is there waiting
to be discovered and conquered.

THE PILGRIMAGE

The man who defends his friends is
never overwhelmed by the storms of life;
he is strong enough to come through difficulties
and to carry on.

THE MANUAL OF THE WARRIOR OF LIGHT

The roller coaster is my life;
life is a fast, dizzying game;
life is a parachute jump;
it's taking chances,
falling over and getting up again; it's
mountaineering;
it's wanting to get to the very top of yourself
and to feel angry and dissatisfied
when you don't manage it.

ELEVEN MINUTES

Those who never take risks
can only see other people's failures.

ELEVEN MINUTES

Waiting hurts. Forgetting hurts.
But not knowing which decision to take
is the worst of sufferings.

**BY THE RIVER PIEDRA
I SAT DOWN AND WEPT**

A threat need not provoke a response
if it is not taken up.

THE PILGRIMAGE

It is necessary to run risks.
We only properly understand the miracle of life
when we allow the unexpected to happen.

**BY THE RIVER PIEDRA
I SAT DOWN AND WEPT**

The heart never suffers
when it goes in search of its dream,
because every moment of the search
is a step towards encountering
God and Eternity.

THE ALCHEMIST

I want to feel the rain on my face,
to smile at men,
to accept all the coffees men might buy for me.
I want to kiss my mother,
tell her I love her, weep in her lap,
unashamed of showing my feelings,
because they were always there
even though I hid them.

VERONIKA DECIDES TO DIE

The two hardest tests on the spiritual road
are the patience to wait for the right moment
and the courage not to be disappointed
with what we encounter.

VERONIKA DECIDES TO DIE

A warrior of light is capable
of understanding the miracle of life,
of fighting to the end for something
in which he believes and, then,
listening to the bells
that the sea sets ringing on the seabed.

THE MANUAL OF THE WARRIOR OF LIGHT

If we pay close attention we will come to realize
that no day is the same as another.
Every morning brings with it a hidden blessing.

UNPUBLISHED

Absolute freedom does not exist;
what does exist is the freedom
to choose anything you like
and then commit yourself to that decision.

THE ZAHIR

It is in enthusiasm for your work
that you will find the gate to Paradise,
the love that transforms
and the choice that leads us to God.

CHRONICLE — TWENTY YEARS ON

Often, during combat,
the warrior of light receives blows
that he was not expecting.
And he realizes that, during a war,
his enemy is bound to win some of the battles.
When this happens,
the warrior of light weeps bitter tears
and rests in order to recover his energies a little.
But he immediately resumes
the battle for his dreams.

MANUAL OF THE WARRIOR OF LIGHT

Before taking any important decision in life,
it is always good to do something slowly.

THE DIARY OF A MAGUS

Start to do something.
That way, time will be an ally, not an enemy.

THE FIFTH MOUNTAIN

I bear many scars,
but I also carry with me moments
that would not have happened
if I had not dared
to go beyond my limits.

CHRONICLE — I'M NOT HAPPY

It is the experience of battle
that strengthens the warrior of light.

MANUAL OF THE WARRIOR OF LIGHT

To fight the Good Fight, we need help.
We need friends, and when our friends
are not near, we must transform solitude
into our principal weapon.

THE DIARY OF A MAGUS

Having the courage
to take the steps we always wanted to take
is the only way to show
that we trust in God.

BRIDA

A warrior of light
knows that he has much to be grateful for.
He was helped in his struggle by the angels;
celestial forces placed each thing in its place,
thus allowing him to give of his best.
That is why, at sunset, he kneels and gives thanks
for the Protective Cloak surrounding him.
His companions say:
"He's so lucky!"
But he knows that "luck" is knowing
how to look around him and
see where his friends are,
those who believe in death
and are therefore capable of living
as if this were their last day on Earth.

THE ZAHIR

A disciple can never imitate
the steps of his guide,
because each of us
has our own way of seeing life,
of coping with difficulties
and with victories.
Teaching is merely showing
that something is possible.
Learning is making something
possible for yourself.

THE DIARY OF A MAGUS

You must be committed
to the place you choose.
A divided kingdom
cannot resist the attacks of its enemies.
A divided human being
cannot face life with dignity.

**BY THE RIVER PIEDRA
I SAT DOWN AND WEPT**

The Mystery

Every day, God gives us, as well as the sun,
a moment when it is possible to change anything
that is causing us unhappiness.
The magic moment
is the moment when a "yes" or a "no"
can change our whole existence.
Every day, we try to pretend
that we do not see that moment,
that it does not exist,
that today is the same as yesterday
and that tomorrow will be the same too.
However, anyone who pays close attention
to his day will discover the magic moment.
It might be hidden in the instant
that we put the key in the door in the morning,
in the moment of silence after supper,
in the thousand and one things
that appear to us to be the same.
This moment exists,
a moment in which all the strength of the stars
flows through us
and allows us to perform miracles.

**BY THE RIVER PIEDRA
I SAT DOWN AND WEPT**

The Lord only demands of us
what is within our capabilities.

THE FIFTH MOUNTAIN

God exists wherever He is allowed to enter.

THE ALCHEMIST

God always offers us a second chance in life.

**BY THE RIVER PIEDRA
I SAT DOWN AND WEPT**

The Lord listens to the prayers
of those who ask to be able to forget hatred,
but is deaf to those who want to flee love.

THE FIFTH MOUNTAIN

We arrive precisely where we need to arrive
because the hand of God always guides
those who follow their path with faith.

THE PILGRIMAGE

Whenever man walks
the path of faith with sincerity,
he becomes capable of
growing closer to God
and capable of miracles.

**BY THE RIVER PIEDRA
I SAT DOWN AND WEPT**

The future belongs to God
and he will reveal it only in
extraordinary circumstances.

THE ALCHEMIST

The best way to serve God
is by going in search of your own dreams.
Only the happy can spread happiness.

**BY THE RIVER PIEDRA
I SAT DOWN AND WEPT**

The best way to plunge into God is through Love.

BRIDA

God's decisions are always mysterious,
but they are always in our favor.

MAKTUB

The Body is the manifestation of God
in the visible world.

BRIDA

God reveals himself in everything,
but the word
is one of his favorite ways of taking action,
because the word is thought
transformed into vibration.
The word has greater power than many rituals.

BRIDA

The warrior knows that the most important words
in all languages are the small words.
YES. LOVE. GOD.
They are words that are easy enough to say
and which fill vast empty spaces.

THE MANUAL OF THE WARRIOR OF LIGHT

Remember that the first direct route to God
is prayer.
The second direct route is joy.

BRIDA

Wherever you want to see the face of God,
you will see it.

THE PILGRIMAGE

There are moments when troubles enter our lives
and we can do nothing to avoid them.
But they are there for a reason.
Only when we have overcome them
will we understand why they were there.

THE FIFTH MOUNTAIN

The warrior of light
knows that intuition is God's alphabet
and he continues listening to the wind
and talking to the stars.

THE MANUAL OF THE WARRIOR OF LIGHT

All energy and all knowledge
come from the same unknown source,
which we usually call God.

THE ZAHIR

Everyone who has the courage
to say what he feels in his heart
is in contact with God.

CHRONICLE — THE TREE AND ITS FRUITS

Now the hands of each person God places a gift
— the means by which He makes Himself
manifest to the world and helps humanity.

BRIDA

When God wants to make someone mad,
he grants all their desires.

THE VALKYRIES

If the warrior of light waits for the ideal moment,
he will never set off;
it requires a touch of madness
to take the next step.

MANUAL OF THE WARRIOR OF LIGHT

We are not alone.
The world is changing,
and we are part of that transformation.
The angels guide and protect us.

THE VALKYRIES

No one should feel afraid of the unknown,
because everyone is capable of achieving
everything he wants and needs.

THE ALCHEMIST

Suffering occurs when we want
other people to love us in the way
that we imagine we want to be loved,
and not in the way that love should manifest itself
— free and untrammeled,
guiding us with its force and driving us on.

THE ZAHIR

The warrior of light
tries to establish what he can truly rely on.
And he always makes sure that
he carries three things with him:
faith, hope and love.

MANUAL OF THE WARRIOR OF LIGHT

It is not explanations that carry us forward;
it is our will to proceed.

BRIDA

When I had nothing to lose,
I had everything.
When I stopped being who I am,
I found myself.

ELEVEN MINUTES

No one can escape his own heart.
That is why it is best to follow its dictates,
so that you are never laid low
by a blow you were not expecting.

THE ALCHEMIST